How to be Really Funny

by

Mark St

PICCADILLY BOOKS
Colorado Springs, Colorado

Cover design by Michael Donahue

The photographs on pages 72, 73, 78 and the top right photo on page 79 were
taken by Neil Sapienza and appeared in *Clown for Circus & Stage* by Mark
Stolzenberg © 1981 Sterling publishing Co., Inc. They have been reprinted by
permission.

Piccadilly Books, Ltd.
P.O. Box 25203
Colorado Springs, CO 80936, USA

International sales and inquiries contact:
EPS
20 Park Drive
Romford Essex RM1 4LH, UK
or
EPS
P.O. Box 1344
Studio City, CA 91614, USA

Library of Congress Cataloging-in-Publication Data
Stolzenberg, Mark.
    How to be really funny / by Mark Stolzenberg.
        p.   cm.
    Originally published: New York: Sterling Pub. Co., c1988.
    Includes index.
    ISBN 0-941599-47-7 (pbk.)
    1. Comedy--Technique. 2. Comedians Portraits. 3. Humorists Portraits.
I. Title.
PN1922.S76 1999
792.7--dc21   99-36766
                                                        CIP

Simultaneously published in Australia, UK, and USA
Printed in USA

CONTENTS

This book is dedicated to Christine DiMario, whose performing genius will be an inspiration to me forever.

Acknowledgments

Thank you, Judy Magee, my wonderful Shakespeare coach, for your help with the chapter, "Fun with Words." Thank you, Vivian Belmont, for helping to create the dinosaur skit. Thank you, Jim Moore, for your special photographs in this book, as follows: Mark Stolzenberg Impersonating Charlie Chaplin (page 74) and the Old Banana Trick (page 65). (Jim Moore is well known for his photographs of comical characters.) Thank you, Toby Circus Ballantine, for the drawing of the slapstick (page 76). Thank you, Neil Sapienza for your photographs borrowed from *Clown for Circus and Stage*. And thank you to the models:

Melissa Van Leer
Jessica Van Leer Viscomi
Katherine Pringle
Marianne Hettinger
Tosso Hettinger
Jennifer Colby
Carolyn Epstein
Brion Black
Vivian Belmont
Marilyn Galfin
Ron Randon

· 1 ·
WHAT'S SO FUNNY?

Funny things make us laugh, and when we laugh, we feel good. That's one reason why funny things and funny people are generally so popular.

Many different kinds of things can be funny. Funny things can be:

silly

serious

cute

ugly

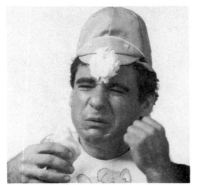

dumb

supersmart

pompous

ridiculous

friendly

gentle

mean   *embarrassing*

and more. Funny things are different, unusual and surprising. They tickle you, excite you and make you think and wonder.

Some things are funny just for you and your friends, and no one else finds them particularly amusing. For example, your friends may laugh when you imitate one of your teachers, but if you did your imitation on national television, it would probably fall flat. It wouldn't be funny because most people wouldn't know your teacher. Likewise, some things are funny just for people in your local town or city or just for people in your country. Other things are funny for everyone—that is, universally funny.

What is funny—and what's not? It's hard to tell. Sometimes you think you've told the funniest joke in the world and no one laughs. You can perform it in front of twenty different kinds of audiences—and no one ever laughs! Then sometimes you'll come up with a line that you're just filling in with and people crack up every time.

The best way—maybe the only way—to see if something is funny is to do it and show it to people. If they laugh or smile, then it's funny. If they don't, it probably isn't.

In comedy, the way you do something can be more important than what you do. A good comedian can tell a bad joke and make it funny. A bad comedian might tell a hilarious joke, but no one will laugh because of the way it's told.

Look at the pictures that follow and see if you can figure out why some are funny and others aren't.

This is not funny.

This is funny.

This is not funny.

This is funny.

This is not funny.

This is funny.

10

This is not funny.

This is funny.

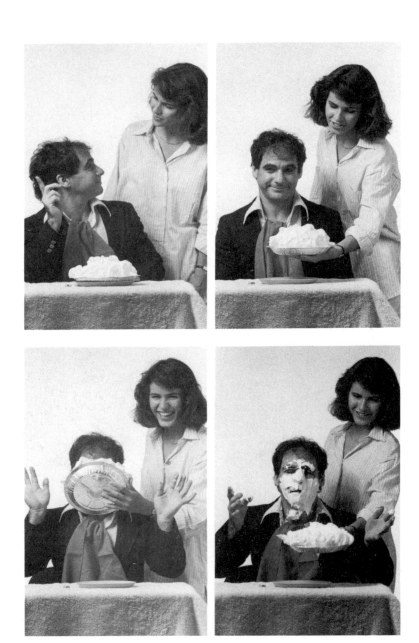

This sequence is always funny.

It is a gift to be a funny person, and it feels good to make people laugh. Funny people are very special, because everyone loves to laugh and be entertained. Great clowns, comedians and actors are loved and respected all over the world. It's difficult to become a professional comedian, but if you're really good and lucky, you may be able to build a career as a funny person.

Lily Tomlin has created a whole family of zany comedy characters—all of them truly original and unusual. Here she is in a shopping cart as the "incredible shrinking woman."

But whether you're going to make a career of it or not, your life will be richer and better if humor has an important place in it. You can use humor in your work (no matter what your job is), with your friends, and simply for yourself.

In this book you'll learn some of the skills that go into becoming a funny person—professionally, in daily life, or just for fun.

These two superstars have very different styles of comedy. Woody Allen's film character is a neurotic intellectual nerd, who is compulsively preoccupied with life's disasters. Eddie Murphy usually plays a boyish, rebellious street character, a trickster who tries to charm his way—and con his way— through life.

· 2 ·
FUN AND GAMES

Warming Up Your Funny Bone

Most people can be funny if they want to be. But they need to relax and let loose to really enjoy their funniness.

One way to explore your funniness is to play some games that help develop your skills and ideas.

MAKE YOURSELF LAUGH

Stand in front of a full-length mirror and try to make yourself laugh. Do anything you want.

You can make silly sounds, talk, do stupid things, put on funny clothes, or act out whatever pops into your head.

Have a good time and try to surprise yourself.

SILLY WALKS

Many funny people do very silly walks. Charlie Chaplin, Jerry Lewis, Groucho Marx and Carol Burnett all have great silly walks that are so distinctive that you immediately think of them when anyone imitates their special moves.

Try walking around the room with a variety of silly walks. Make each one different—some fast, some slow, some bouncy, some soft and oozy, some quick and sharp. Use your entire body from head to toe, and don't forget to have fun.

Give your silly walk a simple pattern, avoiding wild, frantic motion. Keep your movements humorous—like a cartoon.

SILLY FACES

Looking into the mirror, make silly faces — as many different ones as you can. Then make a silly face to go with each of the following words:

Happy	Angry
Sad	Afraid
Smart	Excited
Dumb	Bored

SILLY SOUNDS

Make a tape of silly sounds and noises. You can talk or sing, yelp or grunt. Then sing the silliest song you know—or make one up. You can yell or whisper, sing high or low, fast and slow. When you're done, make up a silly voice to go with each silly face you made.

FUNNY PHOTOS

Take photographs of your friends and try to make them as funny as possible. You can dress them up in weird clothes, if they like. Then show the photos around. Sometimes only you and your friends will find them funny, but if lots of other people laugh too, you'll know that you've stumbled on some fantastic funniness.

Funny bone getting warm? Good! There are other games that will unleash your funniness. Read on.

18

· 3 ·
FUN WITHOUT WORDS

We all communicate with our bodies all the time. We show:

determination   *confusion*

anger   *fear*

and lots more. Whenever we talk, we use our bodies to help us get our ideas across.

20

It is also helpful to use your body when you want to be funny. In fact, some of the funniest people of all time never spoke a word, performing in silent movies.

(Top left) Harold Lloyd is really hanging from this clock. A very acrobatic clown, he specialized in performing crazy stunts. (Top right) Buster Keaton, famous for his deadpan (expressionless) face, also created great acrobatic stunts and gags. (Below) Charlie Chaplin was a genius at using his props and sets in a comical way. In this famous scene from Modern Times, *he identifies with a machine and takes on its personality.*

Performing without words helps you learn some of the basic principles of comedy. When you have to use your body to communicate your ideas, you find ways to express yourself more clearly and completely, and you get much funnier than you were before.

You could spend a lifetime studying the art of "silent performing" and "mime" (some people do), but in this chapter, you'll get just a few basic suggestions about how to get started using your body to communicate comedy and get laughs.

Using Your Entire Body

When you use your entire body, your face, your arms and legs, your hips, your chest—every part of you—is involved in getting your idea across. As you get more active, your emotions grow bigger and fuller, and the audience understands you better.

Look at the difference it makes:

A statue for "HAPPY"

without using the entire body

using the entire body

A statue for "SAD"

without using the entire body

using the entire body

Try creating your own statues for the following:

MEAN	CRAZY
SOPHISTICATED	MISCHIEVOUS
SHY	HUNGRY
LONELY	FEARFUL

Check the mirror to make sure you're using your face, your chest, your hips, your arms and legs. Keep your entire body working all the time.

Funny Faces

It's important for your face to be expressive if you want to be funny. But most of us learn *not* to show what we're feeling in everyday life, and that's a habit it's hard to break.

In this section, you'll find some exercises that will help you loosen up and perform with your face.

(Left) *Harpo Marx never spoke in Marx Brothers movies. His expressive face helped him to create a foolish, mischievous character.* (Right) *Sid Caesar did silent and verbal comedy. His rubbery face reflects his wacky, explosive personality.*

OPENING UP YOUR FACE

Make your face as wide and open as you can.

Now scrunch it up into a little point.

Make your face wide again and then scrunch it up again. Repeat this several times. Do it quickly a few times and then slowly.

24

WARMING UP YOUR FACE

Relax your face and do the following:

Lift your eyebrows without moving anything else.

Now move just your mouth up.

Move your eyebrows down.

Move your mouth down.

Repeat this sequence faster several times: Eyebrows up, mouth up, eyebrows down, mouth down.

Now that your funny face is warmed up and ready to frolic, try the following funny face feats. (Don't copy my face exactly, but try to do these faces in your own peculiar funny way.)

"I'm a bad boy!"

"Ouch, that hurts!"

Use just your face to communicate the following:

"Who do you think you are?!"
"Oooooh! That's disgusting!"
"I don't believe it!"
"That's incredible!"
"I couldn't care less!"
"I can't remember."
"Isn't she beautiful!"
"You handsome devil you!"
"Pretty please!"

Gestures

A gesture is a movement of the body—especially a movement of the arms or legs—to express an idea, feeling or attitude. Here are some examples of gestures:

26

"You—"

"—get out of here!"

"Darn! I forgot my lunch!"

We use gestures all the time when we speak, and most funny people are particularly good at gesturing.

In this section, we'll use gestures instead of words. Look at the following communication:

"Excuse me."

"I forgot my suspenders. Do you have an extra pair?"

27

"Do I look like I have an extra pair?"   *"Shucks, what am I going to do?"*

Make sure your gestures are definite and clear. Rehearse them so that you know precisely what you're going to do and when you're going to do it. Your gestures should be big enough for your audience to see.

When you're on stage, sometimes you have to "cheat" so that the audience can see what you're doing. This means that you may have to keep your body turned towards the audience so that your gestures and face are visible, even if it's not exactly the most natural way to stand. Sometimes it means you don't look directly at the person you're on stage with.

On the next page: two different ways to shake hands.

Playing with Rhythm

There are three basic rhythms in comedy: slow motion, staccato and stillness.

In slow motion, you gesture or move your body at one constant slow speed with no hesitating, no sharp movements and no stops in the action. It's like moving under water. Jack Benny used to get big laughs when

28

SHAKING HANDS

If you look directly at the person you're shaking hands with, the audience is going to miss quite a bit of your facial expressions and body language.

If you "open up" your gestures and body position, it may be "cheating," but the audience will see what you're up to. This is especially important when you perform silently.

he moved his head slowly toward the audience, and then slowly placed his hand on his cheek as if to say, "Well, now I've seen everything."

In "staccato," you move like a robot—very sharply and quickly and then freeze. All the silent comedians use staccato movements to show surprise.

In "stillness" you don't move at all. You just hold still. Comedians sometimes use stillness to show anger. You've probably seen Tommy Smothers use it when his brother asks him questions that he can't answer.

Try the following gestures in each one of the three rhythms: slow motion, staccato and stillness.
"Come here."
"Look over here."
"You go first."
"I am the best."

Now try combining different rhythms in each gesture. You might start off slowly and then suddenly move sharply and then freeze. See if you can mix speeds and rhythms to create surprises. Surprises in the rhythm will help you to be funny. The way you perform your gestures—and the situations you perform them *in*—will determine whether they're funny or not.

More Silent Silliness

Act out the following situations without words. Use your entire body, your face, gestures. Remember to experiment with rhythms and try to create surprises with them. Open up your movements and gestures so that your audience can see you clearly.

After you practice these improvisations on your own, try them out on other people to see if they understand what you're doing and think it's funny.

1. Read a magazine while you wait for the dentist.
2. Try to fix an easel so that it stands—but it keeps falling.
3. Try on a pair of shoes that are too small.
4. Find a big bill on the floor.

FOR TWO OR MORE

1. Give a flower to your girlfriend or boyfriend. She or he kisses you and you faint.
2. Act out burglarizing a house with a very clumsy friend.
3. Discover a treasure chest with a greedy partner.

· 4 ·
FUN WITH
WORDS

We've all heard Robin Williams, as the television character Mork in *Mork & Mindy*, exclaim, "Nah-nooh, nah nooh, nah nooh," or Curly of the Three Stooges shriek, "Wub, wub, wub, wubb, wubb . . ." or Lou Costello scream, "Haaaaaaay, Aaaaabah-tt!"

Robin Williams (top left) is very quick with words and wit and can talk himself out of any jam. In contrast, Curly (top right) of the Three Stooges and Lou Costello (bottom) are slow to react and apt to stammer and stutter when faced with any difficult situation.

These three comics all have fun with words, and that's one of the reasons why they're so funny.

To have fun with words, you can play with the pitch, the tempo, the timing, the volume and the stress of words, phrases, sentences—and even paragraphs! In general, it's always a good idea to color your words and make them musical. But take it further—experiment. You can use nonsense words or gibberish to help you create comedy and get laughs.

Playing with Pitch

Pitch refers to the high or low tone of a sound. When you want to be funny, you can vary the pitch of what you say—any part of it—from a high squeak to a low groan. You can do it with a part of a word, a word, a phrase, a sentence or a whole speech.

Very high and very low sounds are often used in comedy. When Lou Costello screeches, "Haaaaaaay, Aaaaabah-tt!" his voice goes way up in pitch.

When Stan Laurel gets upset and cries like a little baby, his voice also goes up very high.

Groucho Marx, on the other hand, mumbles insults and jokes using a very low pitch. He often does scenes with a big woman, Margaret Dumont, who has a very high-pitched voice. The contrast between them is funny.

Margaret Dumont played a high-society woman in several Marx Brothers films. She always treated Groucho as if he were a gentleman, even though he behaved like a fool.

Play with pitch in the following sentences. First say them in a high voice and then in a low voice. Try going from a high pitch to a low pitch, and then from a low pitch to a high pitch in the middle of words and sentences.

"Doesn't anyone want to play tennis?"

"Who are you?"

"You must be kidding!"

"Which way did they go?"

"I sometimes wonder about you."

Playing with Tempo

Tempo refers to the speed with which you say something: fast, slow or some combination of speeds.

(Left) Comedy team George Burns and Gracie Allen: Gracie talked quickly and nervously, while George spoke slowly and calmly and puffed away at his cigar. (Right) Oliver Hardy talked ever so slowly and carefully when he tried to explain something to his stupid friend Stan Laurel.

Play with the tempo of the following lines. Try them fast and then slow. Make some words quick and snappy, others long and oozy, like: "And a-waaaaay we go!" Now try these:
   "What are you doing here?"
   "I hope I never see you again."
   "Holy cow! Look at that!"

Playing with Volume

Words can be screamed loudly or spoken ever so softly and gently. A sentence may start softly and end in a shriek. Jackie Gleason in *The Honeymooners* exploded with, "ALLLLLLLRIIIIIIGHT!" or "Bang-zooooom—

35

to the moon, Alice!" These words were spoken extremely loudly, which helped to make them funny.

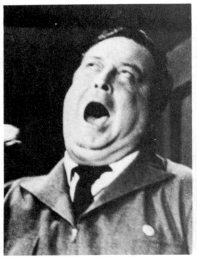

(Left) Jackie Gleason would let friends and loved ones have it with a roar. Stan Laurel (right), usually a victim, rarely lost his temper or raised his voice.

On the other hand, Stan Laurel, after causing inhuman destruction, often whimpered ever so quietly, "I didn't mean to do it—it was an accident." The low volume of his voice made him seem like a little kid, and that helped make it funny.

Playing with Stress

To stress a word or sentence means to emphasize it. We do this all the time when we speak. By stressing certain words, we change the meaning of what we're saying, and by putting the stress in an odd place, we also make things funny.

Say the following sentence with the stress on the underlined word:

36

Doesn't anyone want to play tennis?
Doesn't anyone want to play tennis?
Doesn't anyone want to play tennis?
Doesn't anyone want to play tennis?
Doesn't anyone want to play tennis?

Playing with Language

You can use baby talk, slang and foreign accents to create your own comic language. Red Skelton, for example (see page 121), played a bum who slurred his sentences and lisped. The cartoon character Elmer Fudd talks like a baby. Bugs Bunny uses slang and a gangsterlike speech pattern.

Peter Sellers and Danny Kaye were masters of foreign accents and dialects. They used a wide variety of them and were very accurate. If you want to use a foreign accent, work it out carefully and then try it out on people of that nationality. They can help you get it right and also make sure you're not going to offend anyone with it. Once you've got the accent down, try it out on other audiences. Accents aren't funny in themselves, but if you're good at them, they can add a great deal to your funniness.

Peter Sellers used a perfect German accent as Dr. Strangelove, the maniacal German scientist. In this photo you can see his sinister gloved hand that had a mind of its own and rose uncontrollably in the Nazi salute.

37

Funny Timing

People talk a lot about comic timing and how important it is. Some lucky people seem to have it naturally. If you're not one of them, timing can be a difficult thing to learn, but you can develop it through practice and experience.

Comic timing actually has to do with pausing before or after a word or gesture. The amount of time you pause is crucial.

For a good example of comic timing, take a look at Bugs Bunny. He pops up out of the rabbit hole, to the amazement of Elmer Fudd, but instead of saying anything, Bugs chews his carrot. At just the right moment, he exclaims, "Ehhh, what's up, Doc?" His timing makes the line funny.

Try experimenting with the old joke on the next page. If you play with the timing, you may be able to get laughs:

"Look up in the sky!"

"It's a bird!"

"It's a plane!"

"It's a . . . bird."

A pause after you react to the bird's droppings, and before you give the line, "It's a bird,"—or during it— should get you laughs. Try the joke on friends. Change the pause each time you do it. See which timing works best.

Now experiment with the timing in these jokes:

1. Slavemaster to Roman galley slaves who have been pulling on oars for hours: "I have some good news for you and some bad news. The good news is: you can have 15 minutes rest. Now for the bad news—At the end of the rest period, the captain wants to go waterskiing."

2. PATIENT: Doctor, you must help me. I can't remember anything.
   DOCTOR: How long has this been going on?
   PATIENT: How long has what been going on?

Playing with Gibberish

Gibberish is made-up nonsense language. You can substitute gibberish for real words and phrases, the way Robin Williams does as Mork ("Nah nooh, nah nooh"), but be sure, when you do it, that you know how the gibberish would translate into English. For example, instead of "Oh, my God!" you might say, "Oooooogle, Doobie Wowwow!"

Practice having a conversation with a friend using only gibberish. Know what you're trying to say in English. Then try creating some skits in gibberish based on the following situations:

1. Two cab drivers argue after a traffic accident.
2. Convince your friend to do your homework.
3. Ask someone out on a date.

When you use gibberish, be aware of the pitch, tempo, timing, volume and stresses. Play with the sounds and have fun.

Sid Caesar and Imogene Coca worked extremely well together. They created hilarious routines based on improvisations—with gibberish, with language, and silently.

Telling Jokes

You don't have to tell jokes in order to be funny. The biggest and best laughs come from a character and situation and not from punchlines.

Now, doing stand-up comedy with a monologue is just about the toughest way to be funny. Almost all stand-up comedians, even the greatest, hire teams of writers to keep feeding them material. You need about 35 jokes for a monologue, and you have to be very sure that your audience is going to have the background to understand all the jokes.

The best joketellers know when to shut up and let their jokes sink in. Jack Benny, one of the great masters of comic timing, got his biggest laughs when he didn't say anything—but just looked.

If you do want to use jokes in your routines, here are a few of the types you'll run into:

QUESTION AND ANSWER JOKES

Did you hear about the cross-eyed teacher?
He couldn't control his pupils.

In this type of joke, you ask a question of the audience and then answer it yourself. Or you can ask a question of a character on stage. This riddle format is one of the most common types of jokes.

Johnny Carson has worked out a nice switch on this kind of joke. He created a "swami" character who sticks an envelope with an answer in it up to his forehead. The swami thinks for a minute (timing) and then comes up with a question to go with the answer. For example:

Answer: Mittens.
Question: What do you get when a cat swallows a ball of wool?

Johnny's swami character is very cute and endearing. The jokes may not be all that funny, but the character, and his masterful timing, make them seem hilarious.

EXAGGERATION JOKES

"That house is so small, the mice are all round-shouldered."

Johnny Carson has also developed a switch on this type of joke. He gets the audience to help him set it up.
"That house is *so small*," he might say.
"How small is it?" shouts the audience.
And then he delivers the joke. The joke appears much funnier than it actually is, because the audience is involved in the absurd exaggeration.

Johnny Carson, probably the most successful talk show host of all time, was greatly influenced by Jack Benny and Bob Hope. Like those masterful predecessors, he knows when to stop talking and pause.

INSULTS AND PUTDOWNS

"Is that your head, or did somebody find a way to grow hair on a meatball?"

Don Rickles is famous for this kind of joke. And it's true that you can get a lot of laughs by knocking other people. But this is a tricky kind of comedy. You can really hurt someone's feelings and do some damage that you don't intend, and this type of humor turns off lots of people. If you want to use some of these jokes, only go after people you're certain can take it, and

43

keep it light. Make sure your tone of voice makes it clear that you're only joking.

DEFINITIONS

Oinkment: What you put on a pig with a sore throat.

Bob Hope is a master at making silly definitions into powerful laugh lines. He turns the definition around like this: "You know what oinkment is, folks —that's what you put on a pig with a sore throat."

Bob Hope popularized the informal joketelling style used by most stand-up comics today. His comedy personality is likeable and friendly, and his delivery is fastpaced, with lots of laugh lines.

STORY JOKES

Then there are the jokes we usually think of—longer pieces that can range from a couple of lines to a long shaggy dog story—the kind you practiced on page 40. Whatever you choose for your act, start with very short, quick jokes that will get your audience warmed up, and let the jokes get longer as you go along.

MUSICAL JOKES

If you like to sing, you might also want to try including jingles or songs in your routines. Danny Kaye was famous for zany songs. If you play a musical instrument you might want to work it into your act, as Victor Borge did with the piano. Experiment—and see what works best for you.

· 5 ·
FOOLING AROUND

One of the best ways to be funny is to "play the fool." There are many famous fools:

Lucille Ball, best known for her television show, I Love Lucy, *played a zany housewife who was always getting into trouble by meddling in her husband's business (Desi Arnaz). No matter how hard she tried to fix things, she always made matters worse.*

Art Carney created the character Ed Norton, who was Ralph Kramden's best buddy in The Honeymooners. *Ed comically annoyed Ralph with his stupidity and dumb remarks. He also used quirky mannerisms and exaggerated gestures. For example, he flailed out his arms whenever he wanted to concentrate. Ed always wore an old hat, a T-shirt and vest, and he spoke with a funny Brooklyn accent.*

Jerry Lewis makes squeaky, squeal-y, stammering sounds when he plays his foolish character, a bumbling, weak, shy, childish klutz. He trips, stumbles and knocks things over. Though he starts out as the underdog, he always comes out on top at the end.

Steve Martin is usually "a wild and crazy guy," as he described himself on Saturday Night Live. *Generally he plays a nerdy, awkward jerk who tries to be charming, cool and dashing.*

47

A fool is usually:

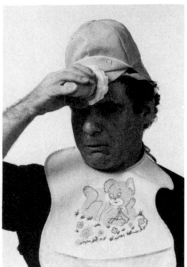

simple-minded—   *childlike*

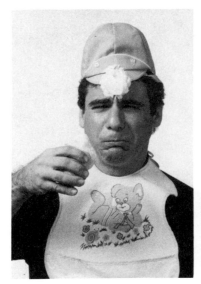

innocent   *and likeable.*

And fools usually have trouble doing things properly. Simple things are very difficult for them, or they do those simple things in different, unusual and difficult ways. Fools are a lot like clowns, but a fool can be any kind of person from everyday life.

Simple-mindedness

Simple-mindedness is a nice way to say stupidity. A simple-minded character might think very slowly, take a long time to make decisions, make lots of mistakes, and repeat the same mistakes over and over, like Stan Laurel. Other types of simple-minded characters might do things too quickly, impulsively and without thinking things through. Steve Martin sometimes plays this type of fool.

A simple-minded fool usually has a limited vocabulary, so if you speak at all, keep it simple. Phrases like, "Oh, my!", "Golly!", "You bet!" and "All right!" are good.

Of course, someone who is like this in real life may be sad or even tragic, but in comedy, we're making fun of all the times we normally feel or act stupid. This is what makes it funny, and everyone understands the joke. In comedy, we don't make fun of really stupid or retarded people. That would be in bad taste and not very funny.

How would a clown or fool get dressed in the morning? Here's one way:

Act out the following activities as your version of a simple-minded fool would do them:

1. Make your bed.
2. Set the supper table.
3. Give directions to someone who is lost.

Childishness and Innocence

Most fools act like children. Whatever they do, they do as if for the first time with wonder, excitement, discovery and enthusiasm. Fools are very emotional and sensitive. They may laugh or cry at the drop of a hat and exaggerate their feelings.

Here's how a fool might try on a new tie in a childlike and innocent way.

Do the following activities in a childlike and innocent way:
1. Recite a nursery rhyme.
2. Eat dinner.
3. Paint a wall.
It helps to study real children (babies, too!) to see how they approach the world with fresh eyes. If you can, spend some time watching them play, and try to use some of those qualities when you play a fool.

Likeability

Fools are usually cute, warm, eager to please and very friendly. This makes them extremely likeable. When you play a fool, you need your audience to like you. Don't ever act vicious or cruel. Fools have a lot of love inside them and want people to like them. If they make a mistake or hurt someone, it's usually accidental. Even W. C. Fields and Don Rickles, who appear to be mean, do not really hurt anyone, so we laugh at them. When Moe, of the Three Stooges, hits Curly over the head with a wrench, we feel free to laugh because we know that Curly is not really hurt.

Here's how a fool might wait on tables:

To please

To charm

To abuse

To impress

Other ways to try: To be accepted, to be nice, to triumph, to keep the job.

Try to be a likeable fool as you do the following:
1. Ask someone to dance.
2. Sell someone a vacuum cleaner.

Foolish Friendships

Fools often perform with a partner or friend who is much smarter. The smart friend, called "the straight man," usually gives the orders and is in charge.

A few famous foolish friendships? Abbott and Costello, Laurel and Hardy, Mork and Mindy, Burns and Allen. There are hundreds more.

The Three Stooges seemed to love each other, even though they were always finding new ways to hit and slap each other. Moe usually was in control and bossed the other two around.

Here's one way a fool and his friend might cook spaghetti. Can you tell which one is the fool and which one is the straight man?

In this case, both are fools. However the woman seems to be more intelligent and in charge. That would make her the straight man.

Now create a foolish friendship with a partner and try the following skits. In each one, decide which one is the straight man and which one the fool.
  1. Deliver groceries.
  2. Report the news.
  3. Sing a duet.

· 6 ·
FUNNY
FOOLISH
CHARACTERS

There is no limit to the kinds of fools that you can develop, and they all can be funny. Just look at the people you see every day, exaggerate their qualities, and you'll come up with some pretty funny original characters. You'll get your ideas from life, but once you get going, you'll want to develop the characters a lot more and give them clearer, more individual personalities.

Making your ideas more specific helps bring your characters to life. It makes them seem more real—not only to the audience, but to you, too. Once you get to know the character you've created, you'll be able to add on all sorts of outrageous mannerisms and actions, and they will make some kind of sense. Instead of being just silly, you'll become truly funny.

Gilda Radner, on Saturday Night Live, *created many hilarious characters. As Rosanne Rosanna Danna, she appeared on the "news" and gave her opinions about everything. Loud and outspoken, this character got involved talking about foolish things—like fuzzballs.*

Many actors create a biography of the characters they play, using their imaginations to come up with a whole life history.

Here are a couple of examples of my own checklists for a couple of original characters I've played:

You can see a funny routine with Al in Chapter 9.

Name: Al Freeman
Play: *Silent Fantasies*
Age: 33
Place of Birth: Under the boardwalk in Coney Island
Place of residence: Queens, New York
Married: to Mildred for 13 years
Occupation: Elementary school gym teacher
Hobbies: Basketball, acting
Goals: Dreams of being a movie star, would like to make more money, wants respect
Favorite color: Blue
Favorite food: Pasta
Family life and friends: Has 3 children aged 5, 7, and 11. Loves his wife.
Loves and hates: Loves eating breakfast. Hates riding the subway
Physical strengths and weaknesses: Ulcer, pot belly, nearsightedness
Quirky Qualities: Likes mayonnaise in his vegetable soup, hates his job, smokes cigars constantly
Miscellaneous: He is currently acting in a weird play in New York but hasn't told his wife about it. She thinks he is going to graduate school.

Yuk—the principal character in the feature film comedy, Luggage of the Gods, *about a lost tribe of cavemen*

Age: 28
Place of Birth: Unja (Canada)
Residence: North Western Canada (in the woods)
Single: His girlfriend, named Hubba, is the prettiest girl in the tribe
Hobbies: Watching airplanes, inventing tools, cave painting
Goals: Discovering something new and exciting to do
Favorite color: Green
Favorite food: Leaves
Family and friends: His parents are dead. He has a best friend named Tull who understands him.
Loves and hates: Loves to draw and paint, loves long walks with Hubba, hates painting portraits of the hunters, hates tribal dances
Quirky qualities: He doesn't fit in with the rest of the tribe; somehow he is different. He is short, unusually curious, hates hunting.
Miscellaneous: Yuk suspects that something exists beyond his tribe's territory and he is extremely curious about it.

Funny characters can range from fantasy figures such as the Coneheads from *Saturday Night Live* or Miss Piggy, to real people that you normally don't think of as funny, like Richard Nixon or historical personages like King Tut. But no matter who they are, it still helps to make up a checklist on them.

John Belushi created many crazy characters on Saturday Night Live. *These photographs demonstrate his versatility. Most of his characters were very gruff and loud and so obnoxious that they became hilarious.*

Carol Burnett is particularly well known for her scrubwoman character, but she created many other oddball characters on her television show, most of them talkative loudmouths. Here she is as an Amazon.

Create a couple of characters of your own, using the character checklist or one of your own. Try to believe in the characters and make them real for yourself.

Now try doing the following activities with one of your characters. Perform the tasks in silly and outrageous ways, but do them as your character would. Add some of the qualities of the fool. (For example, keep making mistakes.)

1. You're late for work and get dressed hurriedly.
2. You're dancing in a disco.
3. Lazily get ready for work. Brush your hair and teeth using your toothbrush for your hair and your hairbrush for your teeth.
4. Try to assemble a toy or machine according to the incredibly difficult instructions.
5. Call someone you have a crush on for a date.

In the next chapter you'll be trying out all kinds of funny actions and props. If you perform with a believable character, all of that "schtick" will be funnier.

· 7 ·
FUNNY
BUSINESS
"SCHTICK"

There are certain routines you can perform or props you can use to get laughs that have been used many times before. These old reliable tricks of the trade are called "schtick" or "business."

When you bring standard schtick into your act, you run the risk of being considered corny and stupid. But if you use it properly, schtick can be hilarious and get great laughs. If your character is funny and your timing is good, then your schtick will probably be funny, too. If your character isn't very real and your timing is poor, even schtick will not save you.

There are two basic types of schtick:
1. funny props and costumes
2. funny actions and bits

Funny Props and Costumes

Many different classic props and costumes are available. Here are a few favorites:

THE RUBBER CHICKEN

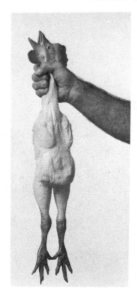 

You can hold a rubber chicken right side up or upside down. It's always funny, no matter what you do with it.

The rubber chicken is probably the best example of a prop used for schtick.

Comedians pull them out of strange places.

They throw them at each other.

They are surprised and frightened by them.

They keep them as pets.

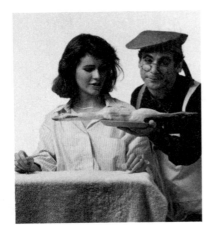

They may even serve a rubber chicken for dinner.

EXPLODING SNAKES AND OTHER PROPS

Exploding snakes take us by surprise. They usually come in a can or some disguised container. Often they are disguised as peanut brittle.

Comedians may give "peanut brittle" to unsuspecting partners whom they want to play tricks on.

The old banana trick: Peel a banana and carefully slice it into sections, leaving it intact. Close up the peel and hold it closed. Then, open the peels one by one, as if the banana had never been peeled before— and react to the fact that it is already sliced.

MAKEUP AND WIGS

Makeup and wigs can help you be funny by accentuating or exaggerating your features. Circus clowns use big red noses and wigs to make them seem silly and stupid.

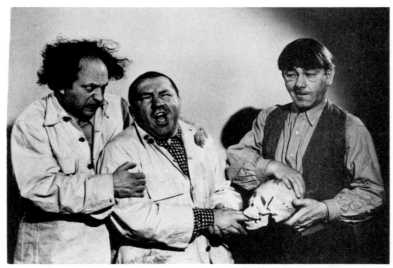

A funny hairdo also helps you get laughs. Just look at the hair of the Three Stooges. Each character has a completely different silly hairdo that expresses his per-

65

sonality. Harpo Marx used a blond wig for his character, which gave him an angelic, impish quality. You can buy all kinds of funny wigs and noses in most magic stores. A particularly funny gimmick is the "fright wig." It stands up and stiffens when the wearer becomes frightened (you manipulate the wig with a hidden string).

Groucho Marx used a thick mustache and heavy eyebrows to express his character's coyness and cuteness.

"WRONG" COSTUMES

Costumes that don't fit properly—or have something wrong with them—can be funny.

A hat might be too big.

A tie might be on crooked.

66

(Left) *A jacket might be too small.* (Right) *Or a shoe might be too tight to get off.*

ABSURD CONTRASTS

Absurd contrasts are funny.

A large full-grown man with a baby's toy is funny.

A small child with a big prop is funny.

A sloppy bum with a distinguished lady is funny.   *A fancy gentleman in a sloppy mess is funny.*

Absurd contrasts are vital to comedy. Some other examples of absurd contrasts:

Mutt and Jeff
An old man in diapers
A big person in a tiny car
A skinny weakling in the boxing ring
    with a big brute

Funny Actions and Bits

MUGGING

This does not mean stealing from people in big cities. When performers "mug," they make silly faces to the audience or to their partner. The silly face is usually an exaggerated expression or reaction of surprise or anger.

TAKES AND DOUBLE TAKES

A take is also an exaggerated reaction. You could do it in response to something you hear, to another performer, to something you see, to something you realize, to anything that affects you. When you do a take, you hold a pose that expresses what you are thinking or feeling. When you exaggerate your reactions, you can be very funny.

Look at these takes:

"Ooooh, that's disgusting!"

(Left) *Huh? What did you say?* (Right) *Did you hear what I heard?*

To do a double take, just follow up your initial take with another take (in the same direction and to the same thing). The second take can be a bigger version of the first one, or express a different feeling or attitude about the same thing.

For example: you see a strange person walk by and do a take—"Oh, I don't believe it—what was that!" Your double take might be "I've never seen anything like that before!" or "That looks just like my mother!"

THE PANTS DROP

Dropping your pants is a very famous, funny bit of schtick—it almost always gets laughs. Just make sure you have some funny underwear on underneath!

The pants drop is a particularly good way to add a surprise at the end of a routine. It's always funny— because it's one of the most embarrassing things that can happen to anyone.

Using Objects and Props in Unusual Ways

Clowns, in particular, are very skillful at changing an ordinary prop or object into something else. A hat may become a friend or an enemy. A toothbrush might become a machine gun. Sitting in a chair might turn into a dangerous flight on a jet plane.

Here Laurel and Hardy use kitchen utensils as instruments.

Charlie Chaplin was great at using props in inventive ways. In the film *The Gold Rush*, he eats a shoe as if it were a gourmet three-course meal. He also does a dance with two potatoes stuck on a fork. He uses his cane very creatively, too. It becomes a third limb and he continually improvises with it.

Whenever you create a skit, try to use everything in sight to help you get what you want, to further the action. Take a good look at the props you're using and see what they remind you of. What is their shape like? What is likely to be available to your character in the present circumstances? Maybe you can put it into the skit and use it in many different ways.

Try improvising with objects around your house. Use each object in three different ways. Just make believe the object is something else and then play with it. You'll find lots of useful schtick this way.

A shoe might be a hairbrush.   *Or a telephone.*

Objects Coming Alive

You've seen a clown dancing with a broom and making believe it's a woman. That's just the beginning of what you can do when you start improvising with props. Any prop can become an enemy, a friend, a monster, a partner, your wife or husband or your boss—if you start relating to it that way. A shoe might be a secret weapon. A lamp might be a pitcher in a baseball game (with you as the batter). A pillow might be your pet, a head of lettuce an evil demon.

Your hat could be someone you love or someone you hate.

Experiment with the objects around you so that they come to life. Create a relationship with the object. Communicate with it. Let it communicate with you. Get emotional about it. This is a very effective way to build fantastic funniness.

One Upmanship—Competition

When two comedians compete for control or try to get even with each other, it can be very funny. Laurel and Hardy were particularly good at this. The competition may build up to an extraordinary fight.

Imitation

You can imitate famous people, friends or partners on stage. When you imitate people you may choose to imitate their voices, their movements, their quirky gestures, their ideas or some combination of all of these. Mimes often imitate people's walks. On the other hand,

73

some comedians, such as the amazing Rich Little, are known for their vocal impersonations.

© *Jim Moore*

(Left) Charlie Chaplin? No, this is the author, Mark Stolzenberg, doing a Chaplin imitation. (Right) Here Rich Little is imitating Richard Nixon. Rich Little is remarkably skilled at impersonating people and imitating their voices.

These are just a few examples of schtick. There are lots more. You can get schtick ideas from clowns at the circus, silent film comedians, shows like *Saturday Night Live* or *The Benny Hill Show*, and famous comedy teams like the Marx Brothers and the Three Stooges. Keep a notebook of schtick ideas that you can refer to when you create routines. Remember that schtick can help you be funny, but you can't depend on it alone. You must have a believable and charming character, funny material, comic timing and a well thought-out presentation. If you're working with a partner, you also need to have a definite relationship between you.

In the next chapter we'll look at a very useful and hilarious form of schtick called "slapstick."

74

· 8 ·
SLAPSTICK

Slapstick is a form of comedy schtick in which chara
ters hit each other, fall down and engage in all sorts of
comical violence. The violence in slapstick is not real,
and we all understand that no one gets hurt. It's all in
fun—like the violence in cartoons. Getting slapped,
tripping and falling down are some of the most basic
elements of comedy.

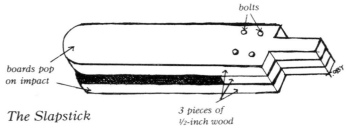

bolts

boards pop
on impact

The Slapstick

3 pieces of
½-inch wood

The term "slapstick" comes from a prop called a slapstick. It consists of two boards joined at a hinge. When
one character swings the slapstick at another, appear-
ing to hit him or her, the slapstick makes a loud pop.

Giving and Taking a Slap

The most basic action in slapstick is the slap. To give a
slap:

Stand next to your partner,
cheating toward the audience.
Measure an arm's length
distance to your partner's face.
Practice swinging your arm as
if to slap your partner, but
stop just before you make
contact. Reverse roles so that
your partner can practice
almost slapping you.

After you've gotten comfortable swinging at each other—and can do it freely without hitting one another—you'll be ready for the next step, which is to show the impact of the slap with your head.

Just at the moment when your partner's hand stops at your face, tuck your head back in a staccato rhythm. This will make it look as if you've really been hit. Practice this on each other until you're comfortable with it. Now clap your hands at your waist just as you tuck your head back. This will give a sound effect for the slap. Make sure it is coordinated with your head going back.

Practice giving and taking slaps until you're both able to perform them easily and smoothly.

(Left) *You might kick your partner in a funny, foolish fashion.* (Right) *Or stomp on the floor near your partner's foot, so it seems you've stepped on his toes.*

Your partner's reaction should always show that he or she has not really been hurt. A funny take to the audience will do the trick. Never give the impression that you're in real pain.

Practice your blows very slowly and carefully so that you can execute them without accidentally hurting each other. It's very important for both performers to know exactly how the blow is going to be executed. Talk it through carefully and get comfortable with each other's movements and timing.

Other blows? A squeeze of the cheek, a bop on the head, a tweak of the nose, a bucket of water on the head, and a pie in the face can all be funny if you perform them safely and in a way that is light and humorous.

Here are some more funny blows:

These are scenes from the classic "Washerwoman" clown routine, in which two males dress up as cleaning ladies and unwittingly get into a very destructive fight. Note that the blow on the left is an "accident," but the one on the right is intended.

(Left) *This tricky little girl is about to bop her unsuspecting teacher with a plastic prop bopper that makes a funny squeak upon contact. You can make your own bopper by gluing a block of foam rubber onto a stick. Spray-paint the foam rubber black or grey.* (Right) *Here is a perfectly executed nose tweak.*

The funniest blows are "accidental" and caused by stupidity of the one doing the hitting. Stan Laurel's character was particularly good at this: Oliver would always get it in the end.

Funny Falls

Falls usually follow a series of slaps or blows and show an escalation of the fight. Practice them on a mat or rug with someone around to supervise you. Never try dangerous falls on your own. Your gym teacher is a good person to help out with this. Falling down is the ultimate degradation, especially if your character is sophisticated, pompous, or an authority figure, such as a policeman, teacher or boss.

When you fall backwards, bend your legs and hit the floor gradually, as in a roll.

Use your arms and hands behind you to stop rolling. Make sure that your butt hits the floor first and not your back or head.

After your fall is over, give a take to the audience or to your partner.

(Left) *You're walking along on your merry way.* (Right) *Hook one foot behind the other so you appear to trip.* (Left) *Fall forward.* (Right) *Break your fall with your arms and hands, like a reverse pushup.*

Make sure that you let the audience know that you're all right with a cute take.

The Chase

Slapstick routines usually have a chase in them. Sometimes a skit ends with a chase offstage, or there may be a chase in the middle of a routine. A chase is any sequence in which one or more characters runs after another character or group of characters and tries to catch them.

When you perform a chase, try to create suspense and surprise by varying the rhythm and timing. The chase should speed up, slow down, and almost stop at some point. The chaser should almost catch up with the chasee, who barely escapes. Here is a classic example of a chase:

CHASE AROUND THE COUCH

A boy and girl sit on the couch.

B = Boy   G = Girl

The boy slides closer to the girl and puts his arms around her. He tries to kiss her.

The girl slides away along the couch.

The boy slides close to her again.

The girl slides away to the very end of the couch.

The boy slides close again.

The girl slides away and falls off of the end of the couch.

The boy stands. The
girl stands.

The boy slowly moves
towards the girl. She
slowly backs away.

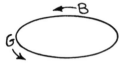

The boy starts to run
after her and she runs
away—around the
couch.

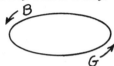

The boy feigns to his
right and the girl
starts to run to her
right.

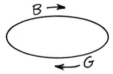

Quickly, the boy feigns
left and the girl runs
left.

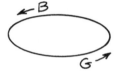

The boy slowly moves
right again as does the
girl, with her eyes
fixed on his every move.

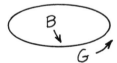

The boy jumps up on
the couch and dives
after her. She gets
away—just barely.

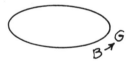

Slowly the boy ap-
proaches her. She
slowly backs away.

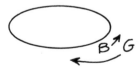

He charges at her and
she escapes under his
legs.

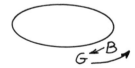

He charges at her
again. Again she es-
capes through his legs.

The boy slowly and with determination approaches the girl. She cautiously backs up.

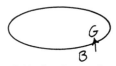

She falls backwards on the couch.

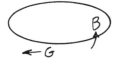

He dives after her, but she escapes.

He slowly approaches her again. She lets him get close. He is about to kiss her but she slaps him.

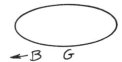

Angrily, he leaves.

She thinks for a moment, misses him, and then chases after him to get him back.

Ideas for Slapstick Skits

Improvise your own slapstick skit. Include slaps or blows, falls, a chase, funny schtick, and a surprise ending.

1. Two painters try to paint the interior of a house. The assistant is a fool and keeps making mistakes. The boss gets angrier and angrier.
2. A silly magic act in which the foolish assistant doesn't do anything properly.
3. For three performers: A wrestling match in which the referee gets most of the punishment.

· 9 ·
FUNNY
IMPROVISATIONS

An improvisation is a game that actors play in order to create new material and skits. In an improvisation there is no script. Performers make up their lines on the spot.

Improvising is like making believe. Children are improvising when they play "house" and other fantasy games in which they act out roles. Many comedy shows, like *Saturday Night Live* and *Monty Python's Flying Circus*, base their skits on improvisations that the actors do in rehearsal. Successful—that is, entertaining and funny—improvisations are written down and scripted into scenes or skits that are used in performance.

In this chapter you'll learn how to improvise, and if some very funny things develop, you can write them into a comedy sketch.

Because improvisations are made up as they go along, they tend to be fresh, lively, and are often hilarious. Or course, they can be serious, too, but for the purposes of this book, you want them humorous and light.

In order to create an improvisation, you need a *character*. You must know what your character wants—*the objective*. And you also need a *situation* to put the character into:

character(s) + objective(s) + situation = improvisation

Character

In chapters 5 and 6, you learned how to create funny foolish characters. These are exactly the kinds of characters you need to use when you improvise. You can experiment with different characters in the same situation and see which character helps to create the funniest improvisation. Experimenting with improvisations will also help you to develop and refine these foolish characters and get to know them better.

Objective

The objective is what the character wants, based on immediate needs and desires. You can make up any objective you want. For example, your character might:

be tired and want to sleep

be hungry and want to eat

Almost any immediate need could work as an objective. For example, your character might be freezing and want a coat—or be lonely and want some company.

Select an objective that will help create problems and comedy in the situation. For instance, let's say the situation is a formal dinner in a fancy restaurant. You might give your character the hiccups and make his objective *to impress his colleagues with his elegance.* To do that, he must get rid of the hiccups. This could lead to some very funny events (see page 88).

Keep your improvisation going by trying all sorts of crazy things to achieve your objective. If one thing doesn't work, try something else—until you have exhausted all the possibilities or achieved your objective. When you improvise, your job is to get what you want (what your character wants), and you can do *anything* to get it.

DIFFERENT WAYS TO STOP THE HICCUPS

Let's say that your character wants to sneak ahead on line at the supermarket. You might:

yell "Fire!"

beg people to let you go ahead

throw money on the floor, and sneak ahead when people go to pick it up.

You can try more far-out ways to get your objective, and the zanier these things are, the funnier it will be.

If your character is being held after school for being bad, but your objective is to get home as soon as possible, you might:

play sick

try to sneak out the door

try to convince the teacher that you are innocent

Other—crazier—ways to achieve your objective? You might fake a suicide attempt, try to convince your teacher that you turn into a werewolf after four o'clock, or pretend you are going insane.

90

URGENCY

When something is urgent, it calls for immediate action. It is pressing NOW. Whenever you improvise, try to make your objective urgent. The stronger and more urgent, the funnier the skit will be. Don't worry about exaggerating. In comedy, exaggeration is what it's all about. For example:

(Left) *This character is starving and wants to eat.* (Right) *This character is starving and wants to eat NOW because he hasn't eaten in two days and this is the last food on earth.*

(Left) *This character wants to make a date with this girl.* (Right) *This character wants to make a date with this girl NOW because he hasn't seen a female for three years and his doctor has told him he will go crazy unless he finds female companionship at once.*

(Left) *This character is afraid he's going to lose his money.*
(Right) *This character is afraid he's going to lose his money, because his house has been robbed 12 times. The robbers are on their way back NOW.*

Make objectives extreme and urgent. This will help your improvisations to be interesting and funny.

Situation

The situation you choose can come from everyday life, since comedy is all around us. You can select any setting. Try these:
1. The waiting area in an airport, where no one speaks the same language.
2. A classroom with a new teacher.
3. A kitchen with inexperienced cooks.

The situation is like a stage set. What makes it funny is the conflict or problem. Let's add a conflict to those situations:
1. You forgot where you left your unicycle.
2. It is the day of final exams and the test is missing.
3. Someone lost the cookbook.

Now let's add urgency:
1. The plane is leaving NOW.

2. The principal is stopping by NOW to check up on the new teacher.
3. The most important restaurant reviewer in the world is out there NOW waiting for his roast duck.

You might want to improvise on these situations:

A couple on their first date: he spent a week's salary on tickets for the hottest show in town. She saw it, hated it.

Someone has taken your table at the restaurant. You must have it, because a spy is dropping off a secret message in two minutes to whomever is sitting there.

You can start an improvisation with this kind of two-person conflict and then if you want, add other characters who either take sides in the conflict or take over. When the improvisation is for only one character, the conflict can be between the character and what he or she wants to do. Try to set up obstacles that will make it difficult for the character to achieve the objective. If, for example, your skit is about an old man cooking spaghetti, it will probably be funnier to make him near-sighted. If it's about an athlete who has to lift something heavy, it will be funnier if he is very weak.

CONFLICTING OBJECTIVES

You can create hilarious comedy by giving your character two equally urgent objectives that conflict with each other. For instance: You are a salesman who is about to close a big deal that you desperately need. But you look out the window and see someone stealing your motorcycle. You don't want to let your customer go, so you try to accomplish both objectives at the same time.

Another example: You are playing in an exciting football game when a ice cream truck stops nearby. You're very hungry because you haven't eaten all day. Just as you're about to take a break to buy the ice cream, the opposing team starts running for a touchdown. You try to stop them, and the ice cream truck starts pulling away. Try stopping both of them at the same time!

Some Funny Improvisations for One Character

Breakfast

(*Prepare for this by filling a large cereal box with five to ten small toys.*)

It's a peaceful Sunday morning and you didn't get anything to eat at all yesterday, so you're really hungry. You bring out a big box of cereal and settle down at the table to eat. But when you reach into the box, all you find are free prizes. Discover each prize—one at a time—and be surprised by them.

Late Again

You are supposed to go and see a movie with your friends as an important homework assignment. If you don't see the film, you'll flunk the course. This is the last day that the film is playing. You have a date with your friends to go to the last showing. You are rushing to get dressed, but can't find one of your shoes.

The Big Date

All your friends are going to the prom, and you are dying to go, too. But you don't have a date, and you must have one in order to get in. You call some friends, but no one will go with you. The first friend is busy. The second thinks you're a jerk. The third is angry at you. Finally you get a wrong number, make friends with the person and then make a date for the prom.

The Weather Report

You are giving a weather report on television when you receive a special bulletin that a tornado is heading straight for the station. You try to inform your listeners (without panicking them), at the same time as you panic and try to collect your belongings and get out of there. You might start dropping things and knocking things over. The weather map could roll up, your pointer break, your wig fall off. You could even pantomime struggling against the wind.

Creating a Skit or Routine

If you come up with an improvisation you like, you can work it into a routine that you can perform regularly. Write down everything you did in the improvisation. These notes are your script. Memorize it. Rehearse it. A good routine requires a lot of practice. Then try it out in front of an audience. Only by doing that can you figure out what is funny and what is not, what works and what doesn't.

When you perform your routine, experiment with different aspects of funniness—the ones we've looked at in earlier chapters: Timing, pacing, pausing in different places, speeding up and slowing down; playing with words and gestures; using silly sounds and silly faces; playing with pitch, stress and volume (if you talk); using your entire body; making sure your character is likeable and foolish; including funny props and schtick.

BREAKFAST

Here is an example of a routine created from the first improvisation. The character is Al Freeman, from the play, *Silent Fantasies*. Al's biographical checklist appears on page 57.

There is soft music in the background. The stage has a small dining table and chair on it. Al shuffles on stage carrying a serving tray with a bowl and spoon.

Yawning, Al sits at the table, realizes there is no food there, and annoyed, gets up and shuffles slowly, sleepily offstage. He returns immediately, and sleepily, with a giant box of cereal. He sits down again and prepares to eat. He's starving.

He realizes that he forgot the milk. He goes offstage and gets it.
He opens the huge box of cereal and tries to pour some out.
Nothing comes out. He checks the box.

He reaches inside and, to his surprise, pulls out a little squeeze
toy—a rubber frog. He reaches inside again, and this time he
pulls out another gift—toy false teeth.

Now he is anxious and annoyed. He reaches into the box and pulls out bunny ears, which he quickly tries on and discards. He reaches into the box again and pulls out a jump rope. He tries it, huffs and puffs a bit, and goes back to hunting for his cereal.

Now he is angry. More frantically and rapidly he reaches in the box and pulls out in rapid succession: sunglasses—a squirt bottle—

Funny underwear—a long clothesline with clothes on it—

And a rubber chicken. He is totally perplexed, exhausted, depressed. He longs for a simple bowl of cornflakes.

Slowly, he reaches into the box again and pulls out a little, tiny plastic bag of cereal. Dumbfounded, he measures the little bag against the huge box. Happily, hungrily, he pours the cornflakes and milk into the bowl and begins to eat.

The lights fade.

MORE IMPROVISATIONS FOR ONE

Here are few more situations for improvisation. In each one, find a specific character and objective, and make the circumstances really urgent. Then pick your favorite and develop it into a routine or skit.

1. You are an alien from another planet, trying to figure out how things in your earth apartment work.
2. You are feeding pigeons in the park and start talking to them about your personal problems.
3. You are a radio talk show host and people call in to ask you questions. Put the callers on a cassette tape. You can make up the questions and do all the voices yourself (use silly ones), or ask friends to record them for you.

· 10 ·
FUNNY IMPROVISATIONS FOR 2 AND MORE

Here you'll work on some of the skills you need in improvising with two or more people.

Listening and Responding

When you improvise with a partner, it is important to take turns: that is, to listen and then respond. When you partner is talking, quiet down and really listen to what he or she is saying. Take a moment to understand and digest it before you answer or respond. When you *really* listen to your partner, your response becomes more believable. Also your audience will have an easier time understanding what is going on.

Of course, there are occasions when you might speak at the same time as your partner, when you want to interrupt, or when you refuse to listen at all—when you're angry, for instance. But in general, listening and responding will help you to develop a relationship with your partner, as well as find the proper timing for your improvisation.

Getting Comfortable

If you and your partner have lots of time to spend together and are able to play tennis or tag, or do some wrestling, that will get you tuned up and working as a team. It will help your improvisations to know each other's movements and patterns better. If you don't have that much time, though, here are a couple of quick games that achieve the same results.

MIRRORS

Face your partner and imitate whatever he or she does. Try to become a mirror image. Let your partner start the movements and you follow. Afterwards, reverse roles. The one who starts the movement needs to do it

slowly enough for the partner to follow. Pick up spee
as you go along.

PLEASE—NO

Play this game with your partner before you work on
more complicated improvisations. It will help develop
a relationship between you. It will help in other ways,
too. You'll feel more comfortable and find it easier to
listen and respond. It will also improve your timing
and add variety to your work. Most comedy sketches
are related to this please-no game, in which one character (who can only say "please") wants something
from the other (who can only say "no"). The "no" character cannot or will not give what the "please" character wants.

This is the way to play the game:

- You don't have to be any particular character. Just
  be yourself. If you like, you can imagine a specific
  situation or place in which the improvisation takes
  place, but you don't have to.
- Person #1 is PLEASE. All that he or she can say is
  the word "please."
- Person #2 is NO. All that he or she can say is the
  word "no."
- The objective of PLEASE is to make NO say "Yes"
  or "All right."
- The objective of NO is to keep saying "no" and not
  give in.
- PLEASE starts the action by saying "please" and
  physically touching NO in some way. You can make
  contact with your partner with any part of the
  body—touch his back, step on her foot, kiss her,
  shake him, etc.
- NO responds by saying "no" and physically moving
  away—taking a step, running off, bending down,
  turning away, etc.

Continue the improvisation until PLEASE gives up or NO gives in and says "yes." PLEASE should try many different ways to get NO to say "Yes," from asking politely or charmingly to begging and crying, insisting and yelling, whining and whimpering, confronting and forcing—whatever you can think of.

Remember to listen and respond to your partner. After you have done the improvisation a few times, try giving yourself a greater sense of urgency by setting up a specific objective or situation. For example: You might say "Please" and be thinking, "Please loan me $200 so I can pay my rent and not lose my apartment." Then make it even more urgent: You're being evicted at that very moment!

You'll find in most improvisations for two there is a please-no game or interaction between the characters—just the way you'll find it in most well written dramatic or comedy scenes from plays and movies.

Building a Relationship

"The Odd Couple," Felix Unger (Tony Randall) and Oscar Madison (Jack Klugman) are best friends who drive each other crazy.

To help make the relationship between your character and your partner believable, you need to know some of the details of your connection with each other. For example, if you're house painters, how long have you been working together? Who's the boss? Do you like each other? Are you friends outside of work?

Fill in the details, just as you did with your character biography in Chapter 6. If your relationship is believable, the skit will be funnier.

Some Improvisations for Two

The Exchange

A customer wants to exchange an item at a department store. The clerk refuses to make the exchange. The customer is like the "please" person and the clerk is like NO. In this improvisation, of course, you would use your full vocabulary. But do keep please-no in mind (in all improvisations).

The Fruit Fight

Two people in a grocery store reach for the same cantaloupe at the same time. It is the last one on the shelf.

It might be a good idea to use a prop cantaloupe that squirts water. Or you could make the cantaloupe out of foam rubber so that you can bop each other with it.

105

Ministry of Silly Walks

Person #1 goes to the National Ministry of Silly Walks to register or copyright some silly walks he has invented. The officer in charge of new copyrights is very critical and doesn't want to register them, claiming they're not original enough. The officer could give Person #1 suggestions about how to make the walks more unique and absurd.

The Animal Trainer

Person #1 plays an animal trainer; person #2 plays the animal (a gorilla, dog, or any animal of your choosing). The trainer puts the animal through all kinds of difficult tricks, and the animal resents being bossed around. Finally the animal rebels and takes charge, making the trainer perform the tricks.

In both the skits on this page, one character is the authority figure and the other is eager to please. This is a good combination for getting laughs. The silly walker (left) is anxious to get his walk approved. The trained rabbit (right) is really trying to do a good job. The authorities are very serious.

106

Let's take a look at the way one of these improvisations might work:

THE DINOSAUR

The Dinosaur is a two-person skit created from the first improvisation on page 105, "The Exchange." It can be performed by two girls, two boys or a boy and a girl. You need the following props:

A bag full of junk (a beer can, a funny hat, old socks, any other silly items you want to include).

A toy dinosaur or other equally ridiculous toy animal.

A table or desk to be used as the "exchange" desk.

The customer hurriedly walks up to the exchange desk in a department store.

CUSTOMER: Excuse me, sir. I have an item I'd like to exchange.

CLERK: Just a minute, just a minute.

CUSTOMER: I only have a few minutes—please, I'm in a hurry.

CLERK: Okay, okay, what is it?

These characters should have conflicting urgent objectives. For example, the customer might make the exchange quickly so she can get home to her sick child. The clerk might want to discourage the exchange because his supervisor will fire him if he takes back too many items.

CUSTOMER: Well, I have this item here—(*She starts unloading her bag of junk on the desk.*)

107

CLERK: Hold it! What are you doing? Get that junk off my desk!

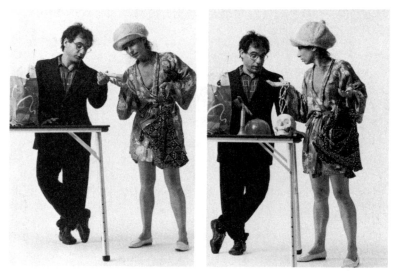

This is a good place to use absurd props and schtick. There is no telling what might be in that bag—the more ridiculous the better.

CUSTOMER (*continuing to unload the bag*): Yes, well, I have this item I wish to exchange—or even better, I'd like my money back.

CLERK (*now very angry*): Will you get that junk off my desk, please!

CUSTOMER: Oh, certainly—(*She piles everything back in the bag and finally finds the item in question, a toy dinosaur.*) Here it is—this ugly thing. I want my money back.

CLERK: Hold on. What's the problem! This is one of our best-selling items.

CUSTOMER: Someone gave it to my child as a gift, and it scares her. I want my money back.

CLERK: First of all, that is *not* an ugly thing. It's a beautiful work of art, and I wish you would treat it with more respect.

108

CUSTOMER: Look, I hate it. It frightens my child and I want it out of my house.

CLERK: Yeah, right. That's why the whole city is waiting on line to buy this adorable creature (*He cuddles the animal*).

The speech patterns of these characters can be very different. The customer is nervous and excited, probably talking quickly and blurting things out. The clerk is more calm, soothing and manipulative. He could speak slower and try to command a certain authority with his voice. He could use a lot of pauses and takes to the audience (A typical take of his might be to think silently, "Do you believe this woman?" or "What a nut!").

CUSTOMER: Look, this is my lunch hour. I don't have time for jokes. Just give me my money back. Here's the receipt.

CLERK: I'm afraid I'm not authorized to give you your money back on this.

CUSTOMER (*crying*): Please, I'm terrified of it and I want it out of my house! Please—just give me my money back. (*She cries even harder.*)

CLERK: Did you follow the instructions on how to use the animal?

109

The crying is an emotional response that is exaggerated to the point where it becomes ridiculous. It's a good way to create comedy. Stan Laurel often used crying to get laughs.

CUSTOMER (*still crying*): No—what instructions?

CLERK: Yes, well—no wonder! You have to follow the instructions. Did you pet the animal?

CUSTOMER: No, I didn't pet it. I hate it.

CLERK: Did you feed it baby food, like it says in the book?

CUSTOMER: No—

CLERK: Did you fill out the birth certificate and everything? Did you give it a name?

CUSTOMER: No—look, it's been terrifying my child and me. We've both been having nightmares. We can't sleep at night. We want it out of the house.

CLERK: Do you sleep with it?

CUSTOMER: Of course not! I don't sleep with animals! What are you saying?

CLERK: You should be ashamed. You're hurting this creature's feelings, poor thing. (*Cuddling dinosaur.*) Poor baby—what's your name? Sid? Oh, what a nice name. (*To* CUSTOMER) See how friendly he is when you talk to him? You can't just plop a work of art

110

down in your house and expect it to work. You have to cultivate a relationship with an item like this—

CUSTOMER: (*cries more feverishly*) I told you I don't want it near me. (*Frantic, hysterical*) It scares me! Get it away from me, please! It's making me a nervous wreck. I can't stand it! Please, please give me my money back! (*She is totally hysterical.*)

CLERK: All right, all right! Here's a credit slip.

CUSTOMER: And those teeth—it has ugly teeth—

CLERK: All right! Just take this credit slip and get another animal—

CUSTOMER (*taking slip, still hysterical*): What's this?

CLERK: It's a credit slip. Now go—go exchange it for another animal—

CUSTOMER (*whimpering now*): I don't want another animal. I hate animals. An animal bit me when I was a little kid—(*Exit, mumbling.*)

CLERK *shakes head in disbelief. Suddenly the dinosaur attacks him.*)

This ending uses the element of surprise. We don't expect the animal to attack him. Try to use surprise at the end of all your skits.

111

Putting on a Comedy Show

You can perform the skits and routines that you work up from this book anywhere—at home, in the class-room or even on stage. But if you want to string to-gether a number of different routines, acts and bits, you need some kind of framework in which to present them. Here is one suggested format for such a show.

THE FUNNYBONE SHOW

A group show that can be performed with five people, ten people, or even a whole class, *The Funnybone Show* can run anywhere from ten to thirty minutes. Similar to such television comedy shows as the classic *Laugh-In* or *Monty Python's Flying Circus*, it consists mostly of one-line jokes, lots of visual comedy and fast action. It's also very silly. This format leaves plenty of room for you to develop your own original comedy char-acters, skits and jokes. Lets just take a look at how you might set up this kind of show:

Goldie Hawn became famous playing a "dumb blonde" in Laugh-In. *She used a high-pitched voice and acted very confused. She gave a kooky laugh when she delivered her lines.*

Opening

Two hosts open the show as a comedy team. They can be characters similar to Abbott and Costello or Burns and Allen, or any other characters you want to create. For now, let's call them Jack and Jill.

112

JACK and JILL come on stage and introduce the show.

JACK: Good evening, everyone, and welcome to—

JILL: The Funnybone Show! We've got a great show lined up for tonight.

JACK: We do?

JILL: Yes, of course . . .

JACK: Say, Jill, did you hear about the fool who goes around saying "no" all the time?

JILL: No.

JACK: Uh, huh. . . .

> *Note: You can continue with about three to five short jokes or stories. Don't forget to experiment with the timing of your delivery.*

JILL: Well—it's time to move on to our Disco.

JACK: Say, Jill, did you hear about the new disco dance for slow learners?

JILL: No, Jack. Why don't you show me?

JACK (*moving his feet*): Dis go there and . . . dis go there.

Make sure you know the details of the team's relationship: How long have they known each other? Are they related? Brother and sister? Husband and wife? Do they like each other? And so on.

113

The Disco

JACK and JILL leave the stage and disco music starts playing. A bunch of crazy characters come out and dance about the stage for ten to fifteen seconds. Then the music stops and everyone freezes, except for one character, who tells a short joke.

Some suggestions for characters: An exotic woman, a bum, a professor, a yuppie, a policeman, some little kids, an old lady— anybody will do. All the characters can tell jokes or just a few of them.

PROFESSOR: Where do all the bugs go in the winter?
BUM: Search me.
PROFESSOR: No, thanks, I just wanted to know.

The music starts again and everyone dances for another ten to fifteen seconds, until they all freeze and another character tells a joke:

SOLDIER: Where were you when the parade went by?
EXOTIC WOMAN: At home waving my hair.
SOLDIER: How strange. Next time try waving your hand.

Running Gag #1

The Disco clears out and the first running gag takes place.

> *Note: A running gag is a short visual joke that repeats unexpectedly throughout the show. In Laugh-In, Arte Johnson, dressed up as a funny-looking old man, rode out on a small tricycle and slowly fell over. He repeated this several times during the show.*

NERVOUS MAN runs onstage, grabs and shakes PSYCHIATRIST.

NERVOUS MAN: Hey, Doc, you've got to help me! It's my wife! She thinks she's a chicken!

PSYCHIATRIST: Well, why don't you bring her to my office?

NERVOUS MAN: Then who'll stay home to sit on the eggs?

The Interview

You may have heard Mel Brooks and Carl Reiner do "The Two-Thousand-Year-Old Man." This interview could be done in a similar style. Do it as an improvisation first and then work it into a skit. It might go something like this:

JACK: Well, Jill, our next guest is here. I can smell her perfume.

JILL: I can smell her, but I can't see her.

JACK: It's the world's only Invisible Lady.

JILL: I see—well, no, I don't.

JACK: Now, don't stare at her. She's very sensitive.

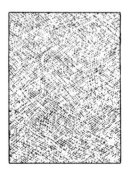

The Invisible Lady—not much to look at. Have a chair on stage for her to sit in. You might make believe you don't know where she is at first. Speak to her in one place and then realize she's somewhere else. You can even bump into her or step on her toe. Finally, she sits in the chair. Put her voice on a tape recorder—through an echo chamber, if possible. Someone offstage can run the tape for you.

JACK: Well, glad you could make it, Miss—what did you say your name was?

INVISIBLE LADY: Crystal. *Ms.* Crystal.

JACK: Yes, well—Ms. uh, Crystal, how long have you been an Invisible Lady?

CRYSTAL: First of all, just for the record, I prefer to be called "a person of no color" rather than an invisible lady. But for the purposes of this interview, you may call me the Invisible *Person,* if it helps you to see things better. . . .

JACK: Well, how long have you been—uh—a person of—uh, invisible?

CRYSTAL: For about 18 months. I woke up one morning and I wasn't there. I looked everywhere.

JACK: Wow! That must have been quite a shock!

CRYSTAL: Well, yes, at first it was. But now that I'm used to it, it feels out-of-sight.

JACK: Do you like being the world's only invisible person?

CRYSTAL: Well, we don't know for sure that I am, do we?

JACK: I guess not. Are there any advantages to being invisible?

CRYSTAL: Oh, yes, a great many. For one thing, I used to have a lot of zits, but now my skin is all cleared up.

And so on.

Other ideas for interviews:
The First Woman to Go to
    Mars
The Sexiest Man on Earth
The Man Who Invented Soap
The Strongest Woman on
    Earth

Running Gag #2

NERVOUS MAN runs onstage, grabs PSYCHIATRIST.

NERVOUS MAN: Hey, Doc, you've got to help me! It's my wife! She thinks she's an elevator!
PSYCHIATRIST: Well, why don't you bring her in to my office?
NERVOUS MAN: I can't! She's stuck between floors!

Rock and Roll Band

> Note: The band should be a spoof of current bands and the performers can lip-sync to a record. They should have outrageous costumes and do all sorts of crazy schtick, like fighting on stage, falling asleep, pulling out strange props—anything crazy and silly that you can think of. You could call them The Disgustings, The Frankenstein Four, Pop and the Weasels, World War II—whatever you like.

JACK AND JILL come back on stage. JILL is wearing a big funny hat.
JACK: What's with the hat, Jill?
JILL: Speaking of psychiatrists, I had to see one because of this hat.

117

JACK: Really?

JILL: No kidding. Every time I wore this hat, I heard music. It was driving me crazy.

JACK: I can't imagine your needing a psychiatrist.

JILL: Well, I told him what was going on and he took the hat and went into another room. He came back a few minutes later and said, "Now try on the hat." So I did, and the music was gone. I was cured—no more music.

JACK: What did he do to the hat?

JILL: Oh, he removed the band.

JACK: I think you need to see somebody about your sense of humor.

JILL: Speaking of bands, we have a special group with us tonight—

JILL introduces the guest rock and roll band.

Running Gag #3

NERVOUS MAN: Hey, Doc, you've got to help me! It's my dog! She thinks she's my wife!

PSYCHIATRIST: Well, take her in to see a vet.

NERVOUS MAN: Then who will I take on my second honeymoon?

Knock-Knock Segment

118

Five to ten characters come out on stage, each carrying a large piece of cardboard, such as oaktag. The oaktag could have the drawing of a window frame on it.

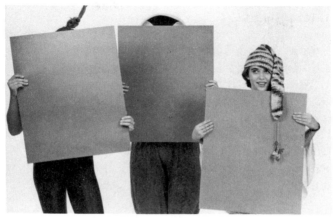

The characters hold the oaktag "window" in front of their faces. Each one takes a turn lifting up the window or pulling the window down and telling a knock-knock joke with one of the other characters. The pacing of the lines should be quick and snappy.

Knock, Knock.
Who's there?
Izzy.
Izzy who?
Izzy come, Izzy go.

And so on for about 10 Knock-Knock jokes. You might finish with:

Knock, Knock.
Who's there?
Acid.
Acid who?
Acid down and be quiet.

119

Sign Off

JACK: Well, I guess that's it, Jill. Show's over, and Jill—you've been a perfect M.C. (*To audience*) That stands for Mental Case.

JILL: Why, thank you, Jack. I know I've been sounding like an idiot, but I have to speak that way so that you can understand me.

JACK: Well, I've enjoyed talking with you. My mind needed the rest.

JILL (*to audience*): I'd tell him to stop acting like a fool, but I don't think he's acting.

JACK *and* JILL: So long, hope you enjoyed the show.

JACK (*exiting with* JILL): Well, let's go. Can I drop you off somewhere—say, the roof?

JILL: Oh, that's funny, Jack. You should go to Hollywood—the walk would do you good. . . .

(*They exit.*)

(Opposite page) *Red Skelton could be funny anywhere.*

· 11 ·
WHERE TO BE FUNNY—SOME TIPS

Just as there are different ways to be funny, there are different situations and places to be funny in. You can be funny with your friends, at school, at home, at parties or on home video. More formally, you can be funny while you give a speech or oral report, in a school play or assembly program, or in a talent show. If you're very good, you can be funny professionally—on stage, in film, and on television. Young people are always needed for commercials, television sit-coms and other shows. If you're really funny, you have a lot going for you.

Know Your Audience

Different audiences find different things funny. Try to figure out what is appropriate for your audience.

WITH YOUR FRIENDS

Everyone likes to crack up their friends. Funny kids get lots of attention and are usually popular. When you're with your friends, the key is to relax and have a good time. This will help your funniness come out.

Your friends probably laugh at peculiar things. You undoubtedly know better than anyone else the kinds of things they laugh at. But a few basic principles usually hold true. Imitations generally work well. Short, silly jokes get better reactions than long stories or sketches. You can find jokes in books (check the joke and riddle section of your bookshop or library), on television, or in movies. Try making up your own jokes. Trial and error is the best way to learn what is funny.

IN THE CLASSROOM

When you're giving an oral report, you can use humor. If you're funny, people will like listening to you and your message will come through much clearer. No one wants to be bored by a long, dull book report or speech. You can use visual aids and schtick in this situation, and your report will go over very well.

One interesting idea is to create a funny character to give the report. For example, say you're giving a talk on nuclear energy. You might want to create a mad scientist character to present it, and use all sorts of funny business. If you're going to do this, it's a good idea to write the report first to make sure that you've got all the facts in it that you need to get a decent grade. Then you'll be sure that you're not getting so carried away with funniness that the report doesn't exist.

It's a good idea to check with your teacher first to make sure that this unusual type of presentation will be acceptable.

When you make a presentation in front of the class, make sure you talk loudly enough for everyone to hear you. If you use an accent, make sure you're speaking clearly enough to be understood.

Another idea for a current events report is to do a "man-on-the-street" interview on a tape recorder. You can interview real people with a current events question or play the various people yourself, making up answers to go with the personalities you create.

123

IN SCHOOL PLAYS AND ASSEMBLY PROGRAMS

If you're up on a big stage, you need to speak very loudly and use large gestures. Color your words by playing with the pitch, volume, stress and timing. When you talk with another character on stage, make sure part of your face is always open to the audience, so that people can see and hear you.

If you create your own props for schtick, make sure they are big enough to be seen.

Oversized props give a cartoon-y appearance and help create comedy. Bill Cosby (pictured here) also inspires cartoon images of his friends—such as Fat Albert—and his family as he imitates their voices, complete with sound effects. His humor is usually family-oriented and he talks about everyday problems. People of all ages appreciate his gentle brand of comedy.

AT HOME AND AT PARTIES

When you entertain at your home or at someone else's—at a party, for instance—try to find a good location for your presentation. If you're going to fall on the floor, you may want to work on a rug. If you're squirting water or creating any kind of mess, a bare floor is better. In any case, always check with the host to make sure your location is all right and clear away any expensive furniture or breakable items.

At parties, you don't have to use very large props or gestures, because you'll be very close to people. However, you do have to speak loudly and clearly since parties are usually noisy and sometimes it's hard to get and keep people's attention. Open your act with something exciting that will get everyone to look at you, like a crazy outfit, wild music or a hilarious prop. Keep your routine short—five or ten minutes is plenty. Just make believe your character is a guest at the party, and you can spend the rest of your time mingling and playing with (or for) one or two people at a time.

You can do a one- or two-minute bit for a few people and then go to another small group at the party and repeat the same bit. When you've reached all the guests, take a break, go back to your dressing area, switch to your next character or costume and start all over. Crazy characters work well at parties. Here are a few possibilities:

A scrubwoman cleaning up the house
A neighbor complaining about the noise
A wild punk type teenager
A circus clown
Harpo or Groucho Marx
A nerd

ON HOME VIDEO

If you have a home video camera, you can experiment in front of it and then observe yourself. This will help you learn about yourself as a performer. On video, you don't have to talk loudly or make large gestures. Even small movements will be picked up by the camera. If you're doing a close-up of your face, the camera will even "read your mind," and show what you're thinking.

A fun thing to try is to create your own goofy commercials—or try a spoof of a soap opera.

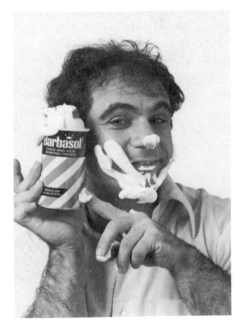

Here is a spoof on a shaving cream commercial. Imagine all the silly things you can do with the shaving cream. Facial expressions are crucial in front of the camera, which picks up and exaggerates your slightest movements. Experiment with big facial expressions and subtle ones.

Another funny idea is to film your family and friends in an ordinary way, let's say, at dinner, but then add a funny narration. For example:

"Here we are on Mars! As you can see, Martians are strange creatures. . . ."

And so on!

Funniness Quiz

When you try to be funny, does your audience:
  a) roll on the floor with laughter
  b) chuckle aloud
  c) giggle and smile
  d) look perplexed and dumbfounded
  e) become solemn and depressed
  f) leave the room nauseated

If your answer is a), then you probably should phone the producer of *Saturday Night Live* as soon as possible to arrange for an audition. If you answered b), you might have a career as a funny person. Keep at it. If your answer is c), you know that you definitely are funny. If you answered d), you haven't caught on yet. Better read this book again. If you answered e), well, perhaps you're meant to appreciate humor and not dole it out. If your answer is f), you might think about getting in touch with the CIA. They may have some use for you as a lethal weapon!

Of course, this quiz is not meant to be taken seriously. However, humor and laughter help us to get through life, to live more fully, happily and healthfully. Whether you're a professional funny person, an amateur comic, or just someone who enjoys a good laugh, your life will be richer if you develop an appreciation for comedy. After all, life is a very funny predicament, and all of us are really funny—no joke!

Index